THIS BOOK BELONGS TO:

____

GOD IS OMNISCIENT.

He knows everything.

He knows the number of stars in the sky.
He also knows the number of hair on your head!

He determines the number of the stars and calls them each by name.
Psalm 147:4

GOD IS LOVE.

He gives undeserving kindness and shows His love by sending His son Jesus to die for our sins.

His love stretches as wide as
the sky and spans from the east
to the west.
Your unfailing love, O LORD, is as vast as
the heavens; your faithfulness reaches
beyond the clouds.
Psalm 36:5

GOD IS OMNIPRESENT.

He is everywhere.
He can see
everything all the time.

Nothing is hidden from Him.
And no creature is hidden from his sight, but all are naked and exposed to the eyes of him to whom we must give account.
Hebrews 4:13

GOD IS OMNIPOTENT.

He is all powerful.

He is even mightier than a blue whale – the world's biggest animal!

Great is our Lord, abundant in power
his understanding is beyond measure.
Psalm 147:5

GOD IS IMMUTABLE.
He never changes.

Our seasons change but He will never change.
Jesus Christ is the same yesterday and today and forever.
Hebrews 13:8

GOD IS JUST.

He is always fair.
He makes the right judgments
every time!

He is the fairest judge in the world.

A God of faithfulness and
without iniquity, just and upright
is He. Deuteronomy 32:4

GOD IS TRUTHFUL.

He never lies.
He always tells the
truth.

He keeps every promise, even His promise to never flood the earth again.
The rainbow that I have put in the sky will be my sign to you and to every living creature on earth. It will remind you that I will keep this promise forever.
Genesis 9:13

GOD IS HOLY.

There is nothing and no one that can compare to God.

There is no one holy like the LORD: there is no one besides you; there is no rock like our God
1 Samuel 2:2

This book is dedicated

to my Lord, my husband, my children, my sister, my cousin and friend.

Romans 1:20-21 inspired this book:

For His invisible attributes, namely, his eternal power and divine nature, have been clearly perceived,
ever since the creation of the world, in the things that have been made.

Psalm 147:5 ESV

Great is our Lord, and abundant in power; His understanding is beyond measure.

Isaiah 40:28 ESV

Have you not known? Have you not heard? The Lord is the everlasting God, the Creator of the ends of the earth. He does not faint or grow weary; His understanding.

Isaiah 40:13-14 ESV

Who has measured the Spirit of the Lord, or what man shows Him His counsel? Whom did He consult, and who made Him understand? Who taught Him the path of justice, and taught Him knowledge, and showed Him the way of understanding?

Hebrews 4:13 ESV

And no creature is hidden from His sight, but all are naked and exposed to the eyes of Him to whom we must give account.

Luke 12:7 ESV

Why, even the hairs of your head are all numbered. Fear not; you are of more value than many sparrows.

www.ingramcontent.com/pod-product-compliance
Ingram Content Group UK Ltd.
Pitfield, Milton Keynes, MK11 3LW, UK
UKRC031203030826
14089UKWH00032B/248

9798869097712